THE GRUMPY SHEPHERD

Written and illustrated by Paddie Devon

ABINGDON PRESS
Nashville

Dedicated to
my four wonderful children,
Kate, Steen, Hanna and Siân-Rachael,
whom I love very much.
G.B.

oK OB

© Paddie Devon 1995

Published in the United States of America
by Abingdon Press, 1995

First published in the U.K. 1995 by Scripture Union

ISBN 0-687-00129-3

Printed and bound in Singapore.

J ORAM was a shepherd who lived in a little house at the bottom of the hills just outside the town of Bethlehem many, many years ago.

JORAM lived alone and was often grumpy.
He moaned and grumbled and walked about
talking to himself as he looked after the sheep.
He complained about this and that. In fact, he
complained about anything at all.

ONE evening it was nearly time for Joram to go to work. "Fed up I am," Joram muttered. "Same old thing every night ... boring, boring, boring ... and it's cold too! Those stupid sheep – why can't they look after themselves anyway!" Joram grumbled on and on, even though there was no one there to hear him.

Up in the hills, the other shepherds were already busy with the sheep. They were lighting a fire to warm themselves and to keep any wild animals away.

Obed nudged Josiah as he noticed Joram plodding his way up the hill towards them, mumbling to himself.

"I see Joram is full of the joys of spring as usual," Obed laughed.

I T was a night just like any other night. The air was still and peaceful. A few stars twinkled in the dark sky above. The shepherds were

busy. They watched their flocks of sheep to stop them straying, and they kept the fire burning brightly. They talked and laughed amongst themselves, and told stories to pass the time.

After an hour or so, grumpy old Joram decided to have a nap. He couldn't be bothered with all that chit-chat!

JORAM snoozed peacefully, wrapped up in his own little dream world ... but suddenly something woke him. Dozily he scrambled to his feet, only half awake. A bright light was dazzling his eyes. He shut them tight, rubbed them, as if to rub the light away... and opened them again. The light was still there, shining down all around the hillside, shining into the eyes of all the shepherds.

What was this? What was happening?

Then ... very slowly ... out from the light, stepped an angel – a *real* angel!

Joram could hardly believe what he was seeing. He could see the frightened faces of the other shepherds who had fallen on their knees in the grass. Joram was not feeling too brave himself. Quickly he crouched on the ground, hiding his face behind his cloak, too scared to come out.

"Don't be afraid, shepherds,
I won't hurt you," said a gentle
voice.

It was the angel!

"My name is Gabriel, and God has
sent me to you ..." Joram peeked round his
cloak – just a little. Obed and Josiah stood
up.

"Tonight in your town, a baby has
been born. His name is Jesus," the angel
announced.

Big deal, thought Joram, still hiding
behind his cloak. Another yowling baby to
keep us all awake!

"You must understand," continued
the angel, "this is a very special baby. He is
the one all God's people have been waiting
for. This baby is your King – your Savior,
Christ the Lord!"

OBED stepped back in amazement at this wonderful news and sat down with a bump on one of his sheep. Just imagine, God had sent his own angel especially to speak to *them!* Wow! The sheep wasn't too interested in this wonderful news. He just felt squashed!

As for Joram, he still couldn't see what all the fuss was about, but he didn't get a chance to ask.

"Go and tell everyone this great news," said Gabriel. "You will find the baby in a stable. He will be wrapped in strips of cloth and lying in a manger."

Gabriel left the shepherds then and rose higher and higher into the sky where he was joined by many, many more angels. Suddenly they started singing and the night was filled with their song ...

> *Glory to God in the highest heaven.*
> *Peace to all God's friends on earth.*

"W-A-O-W!" yelled Obed to Josiah. "This must be the most amazing and joyful night of all nights! We must go quickly and find our Savior. Come on, Joram! Let's go!"

THE shepherds left their flocks and hurried down the hill towards Bethlehem. They've gone mad, thought Joram, quite mad! Running all the way to town at this time of night? And what about the stupid sheep?

"Oh, for goodness sake," he grumbled – but there was no one left to listen to him.

"Wait for me! I'm coming!" he screeched crossly and off he pelted, tripping over another poor sheep in his rush to catch up.

Joram finally caught up with the others at the edge of town, puffing and panting and hardly able to catch his breath.

"Come on, Joram, this is no time to dilly-dally – we're going to see our *King!*" Josiah yelled excitedly.

"DILLY-DALLY? Dilly-dally?" shouted Joram furiously. "I've just sprinted across three fields, jumped two streams and climbed four fences – and you tell me not to dilly-dally! I'm dead beat!"

Josiah tried not to giggle at the red-faced Joram.

"Anyway, Josiah, have a bit of common sense," went on Joram. "What sort of king sleeps in a manger?

That's crazy! A manger's a wooden box that holds hay – not babies – and certainly not kings! I'll believe it when I see it," he snapped.

"Come on, my grumpy friend," laughed Josiah, as he put his arm around Joram. "You can't put us off! After all, it's what the angel told us."

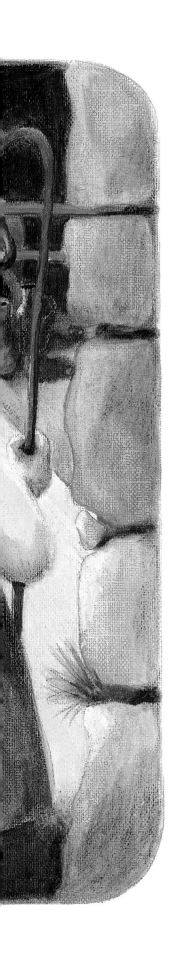

THE stable was not hard to find because the brightest star the shepherds had ever seen lit up the sky just above it. As they made for the door even Joram could feel his heart thumping.

It was Josiah who finally pushed the door open. It creaked loudly. A man and woman, resting on the straw, looked up and smiled warmly, inviting the shepherds inside.

They all shuffled into the stable, past a donkey, a cow, and two snuffly goats, who were very interested in Joram's sandals!

"I AM Joseph, and this is my wife Mary," said the man, standing up to greet the shepherds. "Have you come to see our son?"

"Eh ... yes. I ... I think so," stuttered Obed, a little unsure now.

"An angel came to us tonight while we were looking after our sheep on the hillside. Gabriel – er, the angel that is – well, he told us that a king had been born in Bethlehem, in a stable. We thought he might be here, here in this stable. Many of us who love God, have been waiting for him for years and years ..." Obed's voice trailed off and he looked at the couple nervously. Joseph and Mary smiled at one another. Quietly, Joseph led the men to where the baby Jesus lay.

As the shepherds saw the face of the baby lying in the manger, they fell on their knees in worship. The tiny face of the child looked at them, and at once they felt a warm glow of love and peace. Even Joram's face softened as he wiped away a small tear with his sleeve.

"My Lord, my King," he whispered, "you *are* here. How could I have doubted it? I look at you and I don't feel lonely or sad any longer. You have taken that away. I have hope and love in my heart ... and you have put it there. Forgive me for being such a grumpy old fool."

Joram cried as he bowed his head and knelt beside the baby in his straw-lined bed. Josiah put his arm around him, but he knew that Joram's tears were tears of joy and not of sadness.

ORAM, Obed, and Josiah smiled at one another as they left the stable. They hurried back through the sleeping town and up the hill to their sheep, singing loudly in praise to God for all they had heard and seen.

Joram led the way, his head thrown back, singing to the stars. Even the sheep could hear him coming!

"DIDN'T know Joram could sing," said Josiah to Obed.

"Nor did the sheep!" Obed grinned back.